ABDUL RAHMAN

Reforming the Crisis Ridden Pakistan

Will Imran Khan Succeed in Making "Naya Pakistan"

"I dedicate this Book to the Cricket Hero and the Newly sworn in PM of Pakistan Imran Khan . Hope he will solve the problems of Pakistan ."

By Abdul Rahman
The Author

Contents

1

Introduction

Pakistan's current Scenario presents very abysmal look which is engulfed by a great number of Challenging Problems which can only be alleviated through thorough understanding and taking the each Political Leadership on board and work on emergency basis as these key problems have really crippled the Peace process , Economy and Diplomatic Relation with the neighboring Countries as well as International community . Pakistan must revisit it Policy stands and engage the think tanks and Scholars to put forward the lasting Solutions to these Problems as Pakistan is confronted with . In order to assess the Crises one by One , We shall start from Water and Electricity :

2

Water ,Energy & Political Crisis

Since Pakistan is an Agricultural Country and it depends too much on the Water for Cultivation and irrigation purposes as well as Producing Hydral Energy at the Same Time. The rising Power Shut downs due to 12 to 18 hours and drying rivers due to Cold and Snow has really paralyzed the real pillars of Agricultural and Industrial Development. The Most affected cities owing Power Outages are Karachi The heart of Pakistan and Faisalabad the Textile Hub. People mostly Industries are compelled to use heavy generators to fulfill the demands with Supply . Where as foreign Investors are reluctant to Invest in the country.

Ever since the PPP and its coalition parties came to power , The country has experienced the crises one after and other as the most challenging issue is political harmony . PPP is also under pressure from its allies as well .Since MQM's role is always aggressive rather than cooperative which really forces The Government to ponder over the Political Crisis .Whereas Punjab the Biggest province of Pakistan is under the control of PML N that is really creating hurdles in setup . As Analysts believe that the country is heading towards Mid Term Elections as it has totally on both Political and Economics fronts as well as in countering Terrorism in The country due to Talibanization in Waziristan , Swat and surroundings .

The NRO (National Reconciliation Ordinance is another Headache for the country since it has been termed as unconstitutional by Supreme Court of Pakistan's Larger Bench . The Opposition also demanding moral resignations from the NRO Beneficiary as they had got amnesty from the cases due to NRO implemented by former Military Dictator General Pervez Musharraf . Furthermore , Nawaz Sharif's Demands for Ending 17th Amendment , transferring powers from President to Prime Minister , Prosecuting Musharraf in Akbar Bugti Murder case , Abolishing the ban on being Prime Minister on 3rd Time .Besides , this The Ashura Bomb blast in Karachi and torching of Bolton market by unidentified assailants has also triggered a war of Words between the Baloch Nationalists and MQM in the Karachi .

3

Sugar and Gas Crisis

The Sugar Crisis is also great blow to the current Governments since there have been country wide Protests for the Shortage of Sugar by the Public . They demanded from the Current democratic government to bring the sugar Crisis to end and ensure the availability of Sugar in the Market but it is very sorry to say that despite giving the false assurances , government has really failed to supply sugar at reasonable rates as Sugar mill Owners have threatened Government to stop the Sugar supply if they were forced .. The utility Stores of Pakistan are supplying Sugar to the Consumers at Government rates but whole Pakistan has no access to Utility Stores as they are in Hundreds and the population is in Crores .The Demand and Supply divide is evident in the current scenario . The Sugar shortage has badly affected the Related industry as such as confectionery , beverages , Restaurants where Sugar is used in tea which is the favorite drink all over the world .

The Gas is the natural resource which is used by many industrial Units mostly Hydral power Stations for Generating

Electricity . The Gas is also used as Fuel in the Houses as well as in CNG Vehicles . Due to increase in the CNG Stations , The Gas supply has decreased and The Demand has increased which has created the problem of Gas load shedding in the Country . Compellingly, The Government decided to close the CNG Stations for Few months in order to fulfill the need of Gas shortage . The closure of CNG Stations created great concerns among the CNG Vehicle owners and at same time the owners suffered great loss of revenue due to closure . At result , there were several Protests against such practice .

4

Security Crisis and Economy

The rising Bomb blast and Suicide bombing incidents has really jolted the very foundation of the country as the incidents caused massive loss of Property and Lives as well as created Chaos and uncertainty for the People . The Suicide Bomb blast have become the order of the day in Peshawar and Waziristan and others parts of the country killing innocent people and children and wounding hundreds in Mosques , churches and Imambargahs thus causing terror among the masses . The extremists also challenged the writ of Government and wanted to establish self Government in Tribal Areas .Such situation was caused due to American Attack on Muslim country and Drone Attacks in the Tribal Areas .

The security risks have crippled the country's Economic base and As result of Terrorist strikes , Karachi Stock Exchange crashed several Times and the currency of Pakistan was devalued as compared to Dollar . The Rupees has slipped from 60 to 85 to Dollar within a year which caused great economic crisis and banks also suffered financial loses . The Pakistan headed to IMF for financial Assistance since its financial reserves started to shrink .

to shrink .

5

Unemployment

The Growing Unemployment and poverty has hit the people and they are compelled to sell their children since they cannot afford to nurture their Near ones . It is very sorry state of matter and irony that No one seems to have come for rescue to these downtrodden People . The disappointment and Discouragement, Nepotism and Favourism , Influential Approach , corruption and Injustice ,and the Political interference in the appointments has really made the youth miserable and they are resorting to suicides and joining notorious gangs and being attracted to street crimes since they are not finding the possible means of Business due to messed up and shrunk Job Markets due to Global financial Recession .

The corruption and Nepotism have reached to a extent that Even Public Service Commission Results are said to have been fabricated on the directives of Political figures in the Power . On the one hand Government says there is ban on the Employments on the other Both PPP and MQM are appointing their Party workers undoubtedly leaving no room for those who are waiting for employment . The Bizarre is that concerned Ministries and Departments are firstly appointing the candidates and then they are advertising the Positions just for formality so that Youth could be kept on false hopes and pacifying them with job advertisements but all in vain .

The youth has started considering such Advertisements as deceptive Measures to cool the Wave of anger among the Youth . Not to speak of Governments jobs , the Ruling coalition parties are interfering in the hiring process of Semi Government , Donor Agencies such WHO , UNDP , UN and Other Social Sector Development and Capacity Development Projects such as Benazir Bhutto Shaheed Youth Development Programme (BBSYDP) , Sindh Rural Support Organization (SRSO) , Sindh Cities Improvement Program (SCIP) , People's Primary Health Care Initiative (PPHI) , Social Protection Unit , Benazir Income Support Programme (BISP) , National Rural Support Programme (NRSP), Sindh Coastal Community Development Programme (SCCDP) and People's Housing Cell . All the higher posts have been conferred upon the bureaucrats whereas hopes are bleak for any competent Person to be employed .

It is worthy to be mentioned here that the Interviews held at Lyari Hospital for various vacancies announced by Health Department Government of Sindh for Establishing Shaheed Benazir Bhutto Medical college @ Lyari in which this scribe was also the unfortunate candidate for one of the Posts . we were kept on waiting for six hours and luckily the time came for the interview , The committee was asking only name and district getting the sheet signed and directed every candidate to leave by saying that your interview is over . All candidates

were very disappointed and dismayed to observe such gestures
.

They are playing havoc with the Lives of Youth but one think they must keep in mind that they are underestimating the power of Youth . If Youth came on roads , they will not be able to stop the storm so for the God's sake don't take examination of our patience . The Process of world bank funded Education Department appoint of PST's , JST's and HST's has already been delayed due to political differences and quota system . Since the Education Department has received the funds from World Bank but still reluctant to issue offer letters . The Whole Process has been politicized deliberately so that it may be delayed to temper with results and marks of candidates . The Sight of employees of forcibly closed Projects moves all of us to tears since it was the only source of Livelihood for them .

The Projects such as Sindh Devolved Social Services Program (SDSSP) , Decentralization Support Programme (DSP) , Decentralized Elementary Education Project (DEEP) , National Commission for Human Development (NCHD) and the last nail in coffin is the National Programme For Improvement of Watercourses (NPIW) whose employees are seen protesting for regularization of their services since they have been serving for last two decades . On the pleas of People and owing to efforts of Social sector companion Nafisa Shah , The NCHD has been restored and all the sacked employed are being called back to join their services . That is good sign since 80000 employees will regain their jobs with the smile on their faces . It will also give them a sigh of relief in the current financial constraints .

Conclusion: If Pakistan wants to get rid of above crises then it must make an strategy to counter terrorism , bring end to Political confrontation since current government has been engulfed with series of Crises and the Crises add fuel to fire to the misery and raise questions for Good governance . Since Pakistan is often dubbed as welfare State but people are yet experience the feeling of being citizens of welfare state . The political imbroglio should be resolved in order save Democracy from being derailed by so called Non state Actors as stated by president of Pakistan .If they are present in Pakistan , they should be brought to book and all the sacked employees of closed projects should be restored like NCHD as they are the real assets for this Land which is really the gift of gab for all of us . We cannot see our paradise left ablaze in hands of extremists and terrorists and bankrupts . Its all over and we need to turn over a new leaf in order to develop in the same pace as its neighboring Countries have developed tom the level and nearing to achieve the Millennium Development Goals .

6

Local Governance and Commissionerate System

Pakistan has been influenced by British colonial rule when it was united with India popularly called the subcontinent . The British raj gave some wonderful systems to be carried over by the successful governments which includes railways , policing , judiciary , land revenue and local governance . Both India and Pakistan have been over influenced by the British colonial rules which are still kept intact as our legislators have not bothered so far to either revise these obsolete laws and acts or produce alternatives to replace those old acts and laws whose efficiency has diminished with passage of time and after advancement in the technology as well as rising population , these laws need amendments and addition of new paras.

However, all laws could not be done away with overnight as enough time will be required to present a well balanced and effective policy to either make any amendments in the laws or devise new ones keeping in view the ever increasing demands of the time .

Keeping in view the ever increasing demand of Local Governance system to make the idea of providing lasting peace , devolving Administrative , Governance , and Financial Powers at District , Tehseels and Union Council levels , General Pervez Mushharraf tasked the NRB Chairman Daniyal Aziz to prepare the Draft of Local Government Ordinance 2001 . Daniyal Aziz along with Committee members consulted the various Public Policy and Governance experts , arranged Seminars and Discussions regarding the proposed Local government Ordinance 2001 and finally getting inputs from all the stake holders finalized the Draft and presented in the assembly for approval which was approved unanimously.

The local bodies System introduced by General Pervez Musharaf gave great Administrative , Financial and Local Governance powers to the People of Districts and City Governments . The People got easy access to Executives at district level and got their queries solved in their Districts which saved their precious time of travelling to Divisional and Provincial Head Quarters for common purposes . It was very first time that Districts were given financial autonomy and Finance and Planning Departments were devolved at district level as 150 Years Old Commissionerate system had no provisions to devolve or decentralize the Financial system to account IV from account –I .

This step greatly helped the various line departments to prepare their budget estimates and get releases from finance and Planning Departments executives . It was also very first time that Police act of British Colonial times was replaced with Police Order 2002 separating Operation and Investigation branches of the police and renaming the Designation of Superintendent of Police as District Police Officer (DPO) working under the supervision of Nazims and District Coordination Officers of grade 20 .

The Commissionerate system was influential in terms of matters related to Governance since it served the purpose of Provincial Governments as powerful control over the Financial , Administrative and Governance Powers considered the people as subjects rather than as equal citizens and had no provision for community Supported Governance where the Communities could have free will and wish to suggest development schemes or Programmes for social ,economic and cultural activities .

The Commissionerate system had long maintained their supremacy in civil services since Indians retained Indian Civil Service but Pakistani elite had named their civil service as Central Superior Service means those who cleared the English dominated Competition were Superiors to the society . Now , if you named them superiors , how would they serve the cause of community who seek lasting solutions to their Problems . They had easily became the Superiors and started considering the poor segments of the society as inferiors . Moreover , these civil servants broke the records of corruption in administrative matters as a result people got sick of them and wanted a new system based on the principle of Justice at the door step , say in the matters related to the community and the matters related to governance , participatory planning and monitoring the working of local administration as well as employees of public or social service departments such as Education , health and Community Development .

The revival of 150 years old obsolete system also served the interests of Political pundits who get posted the District Executives such as Deputy Commissioners , Superintendents of Police ,Assistant Commissioners (AC's), Mukhtiarkars of revenue , District Educations Officers and even Station House Officers SHO's of their choice so that they may maintain their influence and dominancy over the District Administration and get their interests served by hook or crook . The District Government Heads such DC's and Police Heads play in hands of powerful Feudals who are at the same time , elected MNA's and MPA, . But the Irony is that in some provinces , the MPA's and MNA's have been given the control of TMA,s and Other Departments to establish their influence and misappropriate the funds meant for the Sanitation , Public Places , Communication and Development .

The Local Bodies System 2001 was no doubt a gift for the people of Pakistan to have been implemented with due attention and making it transparent through some amendments . The USAID , ADB , World Bank and AusAid had pledged great support for improvement and sustainability of the system . The Programmes such as Sindh Devolved Social services Program SDSSP , Decentralization Support Program by ADB , Districts that work by USAID and Devolution Trust for Community Empowerment were the prominent Programmes which provided Financial Grants to Districts , Capacity Building of Officers of District Governments , Budgetary Consultative Workshops , revenue generation at District Level , Tax , OZT Collection etc . These wonderful programmes also helped the districts to devise Policies and Standard Operating Procedures (SOP's) and Governance Reforms by training the Nazims , Naib Nazims , Councilors and Officers of the District .

The Local Governance Ordinance of 2001 had also introduced new departments at district level such as Civil Defense , Law Department , IT Department ,Finance and Planning Department along with Old Departments of Education , Health

, Revenue , Agriculture , Food and Works and Services ,Community Development Departments headed by EDO's and DO's and DDO's etc . Though the number of Executive bureaucrats was maximized but it served the interests of the public and who got their issues solved by approaching the concerned departments of District .

It would be interesting to know that schemes such as crosses , brick pavements and CC Blocks or Drains were approved locally by the Union council Nazims or Tehseel Nazims which gave relief to the public where as in commissionerate system Deputy Commissioners have been given three Millions Annually for Operational and Grant in Aid purposes which is really insufficient amount at the disposal of Deputy Commissioners to serve the needy people submitting appeals to the District Executive . Where as in Local Bodies District Coordination Officers had 2 Billion Rupees at their Disposal in terms of Salary , non salary , grant in aid and Development purposes . At the same time they had complete financial autonomy since funds were placed at district Governments Account-IV released by DCO's , EDO's Finance and Planning through District Accounts Officers . There was great check and balance over the release of funds and their proper utilization since monthly utilization and internal audit provision in each department of District .

The Union Council were provided 100000 to 200000 lac per month for development and salary purposes . Tehseel and District Nazims were preparing the Annual budgets themselves with help of Finance and Planning Departments with budget estimates from all the departments through DDO's . This greatly helped the Elected representative of the Taluka and District councils to learn the legislative and governance dynamics at grassroots level .

This greatly encouraged community empowerment through engagement in development and Financial planning for the communities who voted them and supported them in non party based elections . Most of the previous Nazisms won the elections in General Elections for MNA' and MPAs since they had been able to groom themselves as Public representatives and the Local Bodies Platform greatly served as nursery for such future Leaders who have been entrusted with duties of Policy Making and Implementation at Provincial and Federal Level .

The Flaws may be related to control of financial components since no watch dogs for monitoring the Executives were available at district level . The check and balance was a bit loose but was not loose at all that it may have been replaced with the Colonial Commissionerate System which heralds that we are not free from the influence of British Raj and we still endorse and sustain the laws and acts made 150 years ago . The World is not the same as it was 150 years ago nor the problems and needs are the same as they were in those days .

So why we get stuck to these oldies why not try the new and improved ones. The System introduced after open discussions and consultations are reversed or replaced on the pretext that it was introduced by Military ruler .A person can be bad due to his behavior but if someone gives you the change with clear road map then it's our duty to appreciate the concept and mould it according to time and consequences rather than making it controversial through useless and averse comments that something was introduced by a dictator . Then the question will pop up in every bodies mind that Commissionerate system was the production of British who occupied your land and made you slaves then commissionerate system must be despised of more than the Local Bodies System of 2001 introduced by Pakistani Soldier .

The previous argument regarding a system introduced by Musharaf ,has no base or weightage since it does not quite satisfy the reason to change the modern Community based approach to One man show at the districts where no public opinion is regarded , no timely relief is provided but the people have been subjugated to obey the orders of the local feudal , DC's , Commissioners with little options but to approach courts for relief .

The Commissionerate system is very old and obsolete may be considered as the dead horse but the Provincial Governments are stuck to it and resurrected it again in worst format which does not serve the interests of common men . Some provinces such as Punjab is running a blend of Local Governance and Commissionerate system which may be good experiment but the other provinces such as KPK , Baluchistan and Specially Sindh has stuck to this dead horse which has held the whole governance system in abeyance .Commissionerate System may have pleased the bureaucrats who seem to have regained their former powers but will continue to haunt the common men by serving the will of feudals and playing in their hands.

It is , therefore , ardent wish of the people to do away with bureaucratic influenced system and introduce the Community participated and represented system to build the confidence and solve the ever growing problems of unemployment , law and order situation , financial constraints and justice at the door steps .This may happen when the leaders of Pakistan specially the provincial leaders will give serious consideration to local Governance issues , community participation and sustainable Development in order to put Pakistan on the right track leading to progress so that the idea of a welfare state could be materialized . After eighteenth amendment , it is mandatory upon the provincial Governments to devolve the Administrative , Financial and Local Governance Powers at District and Union Council level to make the dream of a brighter Pakistan a reality.

References:

1. Local government system in Sind: includes Sind Local Government Ordinance, 1979.

By Sind (Pakistan). Sind Local Government Board.; Book : State or province government publication ,Language: English Publisher: [Karachi] : Sind Local Govt. Board, 1981

2. Local government system in Sind. By Sind (Pakistan).;

Book: State or province government Publication, Language: English, Publisher: [Karachi] :

Sind Local Govt. Board, 1981

3. Mahmood Ali Shah :*Sardari, jirga & local government systems in Baluchistan*

' Book, Language: English Publisher: Quetta: Qasim Printers, 1992.

4. Munawwar Alam :*An introduction to the local councils system in Sindh & elections* United Nations Development Programme.; Norway. Direktoratet for utviklingshjelp. Book Language: English, Publisher: Islamabad : Electoral Processes Resource Centre, 1999.

5. Munawwar Alam *: Managing change in local governance* Andrew Nickson; , Book Language: English ,Publisher: London,

U.K. : Commonwealth Secretariat, 2006.

6. *The Sindh **Local Government Ordinance, 2001***

7. Amended Up To December 27, 2002 ,Chapters related

Governance and Administration
  8. The Sindh Local Government Act, 2013
  http://www.sindh.gov.pk/dpt/Local%20Government/
  THE%20DRAFT%20SINDH%20LOCAL%20GOVERNMENT%
  20ACT%202013.pdf

7

Challenges Before New PM Imran Khan

With PTI Emerging as single Majority Party having more than 115 NA seats and More than 124 PA seats in Punjab, 65 PA seats in KP and Second Major Party in Sindh with 22 PA Seats, PTI Chairman is well prepared to be the Prime Minister of Pakistan. The Idea of "Naya Pakistan" worked and people left their comfort zone and voted for change. After, overall seat analysis, PTI is well in position to form Government in Center, Punjab and KP.While PML-N 62 NA Seats , 130 PA seats of Punjab and PPP as third with 39 NA seats and 68 PA seats of Sindh and will like form government in Sindh .

Furthermore , PTI will sit on Opposition benches in Sindh possibly giving tough time to PPPP to improve their performance Since MQM was bit humble or friendly with PPP as the City Mayor Belonged to their Party in the previous tenure . In today's Public address, PTI Chief (Future PM) said that he was the only leader ever to be targeted personally but buried all rifts , the differences and has completely wiped out his Past differences with people. He further clarified that he will not pursue the Policy of Victimization either.

He projected his clear vision that he will establish close brotherly relations with All the major Islamic Countries Especially Saudi Arabia, Iran, Turkey and will play his role to diffuse tensions between Saudi Arab and Iran. He stressed that the rule of law to be the top priority before his Government.He was reported as saying that PTI government will focus on Education, Health, Police Reforms, Job creation, Fiscal Policy, Foreign Policy and Best Governance Model that suits the Democratic Trend and the Model of Pakistan. He specially hinted to involve 200 Pakistanis working abroad to reform the institutions to be made functional on modern Lines.

The first Challenge to PTI is the implementation of Uniform Education Policy in all the four provinces. It is suggested that Education to be made Federal Subject to have uniformity in Curriculum and its foundation on international Standards. Secondly, the promotion of Scientific Research and Technology in all the Four provinces including GB. The Establishment of New Universities throughout Pakistan in the Lines of NAMAL college Mianwali. The Scholarships many be offered to the Deserving students so that they may face the problem of lack Funds for Studies. Establishing and creating Job Markets so that the university graduates may not face problem in getting jobs. Offering Scholarships for M.Phil and Ph.D Members of public Universities as well as for the talented Students to further their research in their respective fields.

The Establishment of New Hospitals in each Taluka Head Quarter and District Head Quarters and up gradation of existing Hospitals and equipping them with Modern facilities. Establishment of Cancer Hospital in every province to facilitate the Cancer patients and ensure their treatment free of Cost. Introducing Health cards or Insurance for the patients with Fatal diseases. The Health insurance will cover their treatment costs. The Energy crisis has been very critical in Pakistan due to Demand and Supply GAP. PTI has to spearhead the Construction of New Dams such as Bhasha and Mohammad Dams since these have been cleared by Chief Justice of Pakistan ,Justice Saquib Nisar that need to be constructed on Public-Private Node.

He even established the Dams Construction Fund. PTI can further the fundraising so that construction work must be started on time. The load-shedding problem is very old even PML-N has not resolved the Load shedding issue. As the PML-N leadership, Nawaz Shareef and Shahbaz Shareef told white lies with the Simple people Pakistan that the issue of Load shedding will be resolved by 2018 but people of Pakistan are still experiencing Load unresolved. PTI has to solve the core issue on war footing basis so that prosperity could be brought in Pakistan and the Textile & Garments Industry of Karachi and Faisalabad could be revitalized.

The third biggest challenge is the depreciation of Rupee against Dollar. The Economist team should be engaged with the composition of Senior and young economists and to do the spade work for viable and sustainable Economic policy. In this connection, the services of Policy Think Tanks specially Sustainable Development Policy Institute (SDPI) Islamabad would be the key to give the best policy advise and great Professional Asad Umar would be Instrumental in this regard as well.

The Fourth Biggest challenge is the devising of Internal policy and Foreign Policy for Pakistan . it is imperative that

Pakistan should adopt a clear foreign Policy and determine new terms of Engagement with US, Russia and our old friend neighbour China. Execution and acceleration of CPEC Projects must improve the Infrastructure of Pakistan.The Fifth biggest challenge is to gain access to International Markets to improve and increase exports of Pakistan such as Grains, Fruits, Textiles and Garments. Establishing Industrial Zones and Economic zones and functioning of Gwadar Port. The Improvement of Communication, Highways, Railways and Airways especially restructuring of PIA and Pakistan Steel.

The Sixth largest challenge is the Governance Model especially the Local Governance. This should be a federal subject so that there should be a uniform local governance Model. The Experts should be engaged to study the standard local Governance Models and adopt or devise the models given needs and requirements local People .There is also the issue of security at Loc with India owing to The Kashmir Dispute. Even the so-called Indian Media dubbed the Victory of Imran Khan as a bad omen for India due to their bonhomie with PML-N. PML-N has always maintained friendly relations with the compromise on the Kashmir. In this connection, PTI initiatives to highlight the issue in the light of UN for its resolution .

If all these issues are resolved, the people of Pakistan will have the positive image about PTI and its visionary leadership. People have trusted PTI leadership and Hopefully, PTI won't breach the trust.

People Voted for the Change and they just want to reap the fruits of change and see Pakistan as the country where the unemployment, security issues, Education issues , Health issues, bad Governance should be wiped as per their Slogan of *Naya Pakistan.*

There should be zero tolerance for corruption and The Institutions such as NAB, ACE and FIA may take action against any person if he is found involved with clear evidence.

There should also be strict laws for Corruption and befitting punishment will be meted out as was done with former PM Nawaz and his Daughter Mariam Safdar and Captain Safdar.

It is clear from their sentence that no matter how powerful the corrupt people are, they would be executed in a similar fashion.

There should be a congenial environment for the Foreign Direct Investment FDI and the boosting of the Hotel and Tourism Industry as done by UAE and Malaysia etc. Hope IK will fulfill his promises and solve the Challenges of Pakistan with dedicated and professional team.

8

Boosting Higher Education Outreach

Education is considered the backbone in shaping the country's Future course of Action. The great nations of the World who have achieved tremendous growth and Success, and emerged as the most developed countries of the world, have especially focused on Education- preferably the Professional Higher Education in the field of Engineering, Medicine, Finance and Planning. The developed nations also have focused on the advancement of Science and technology-based education and bridged the gaps in Educational outreach.

The countries like Japan, China, Malaysia, Singapore, Indonesia, America, Australia, and England have reached the heights of Success through Education. The Average Literacy rates in these countries are above 90% as compared to other countries.

The Developed nations of the World have brought many innovations in education, Information and Communication Technologies and built advanced governance System and E-Government Initiatives. Such initiatives have eased the process of Education outreach. The online infrastructure of these developed nations have prompted the developing nations like Pakistan to learn from these countries and improve the Education Information Technologies and improve the Education Standards from Primary to Secondary, and from College Education to University Education. The Higher Education Commission (HEC) formerly the University Grants Commission (UGC) has played a vital role in building linkages between the universities in lieu of Research and Academic Excellence. Especially the former HEC Chairman Dr Atta-ur-Rahman' tenure is considered the golden era for Improving the spectrum of Research industries and Capacity Building of The Universities and Degree awarding Institutes DAI's. He also set the SOP's of HEC and made it a Central regulatory Body of Higher Education Institutes and Introduced the ranking system in the Universities to improve the quality of education and promoted research-oriented Education at Graduate and Post Gradual level .

Despite all this, the higher Education outreach is still the far cry for rural population as there is a great dearth of Higher Education Institutes in Rural areas of Pakistan.Even the existing Institutes in the Rural areas are not imparting the Modern Education since the same obsolete type of Teaching Methodology is adopted in these Institutes. Even at the Degree Colleges fall short in imparting standardized Education on Modern lines as being offered at the Reputed Institutes .

As a result, the number of Graduates produced by Rural Area Institutes per year , is too big but their Skills are not the same as compared to the Graduates of Urban Area Institutes. The Reasons are several but the main reasons are the lack of modern laboratories, lack of ICT based facilities, lack highly qualified Faculty and Trained Administrative & Managerial Staff to boost the academic Excellence of the Institution and transform it into an Ideal Institute to set the precedence for those who follow.

The Rural and Urban Divide has also divided the quality of Education imparted and the degrees are offered at District and Tehseel Level. If we speak of Sindh only, the virus of Copy Culture have plagued the very roots of our Degree Level education and the Production is very substandard.so much so ,that the college graduates are not able to clear the Entry tests of various universities to pursue Master Level Studies .

Unfortunately, the situation becomes miserable when we come to know that in Sindh and Other Provinces, there are only Degree colleges for Science Students offering Regular Admissions in F.Sc Pre-Medical and Pre-Engineering Groups whereas limited admissions are offered to Arts or Humanities Students at Tehseel Level. In Addition to these, the affiliated colleges also offer regular Admissions in B.Sc and B.A but apart from the colleges of Big Cities, the attendance Ratio in Rural or Tehseel Level is very nominal and the classes are not run properly for such Degree Level students due to various reasons such lack of required Staff , Syllabus and Books ,funds and the interest of Students due to socio Economic Conditions .
Ironically, students without guidance and career counseling take admissions either by Parents Wish or on their own preferably in Engineering and Medical Groups but they do not know that there are other fields such as commerce, computer science and Fine Arts for Intermediate Students to opt for if they are willing to take admissions in these groups other than

traditional pre-Engineering and Pre-Medical groups. The main reason is that there is no any college at Tehseel or District Level to offer Commerce, Computer Science and Fine Arts in Sindh . Compellingly, most of the students seek admissions at Science Colleges as they donot have alternate Options.

The Education in Punjab is considered more standard as compared to other provinces since in Punjab, every college offers admissions in Pre-Engineering, Pre-Medical, Commerce, Fine Arts and Computer Science. Even their degree Classes are standardized and faculty is also efficient to impart quality based Education . The Education in KP has been improved tremendously under current PTI regime specially they have focused the Secondary Education and College Education . Even Baluchistan has improved Education Spectrum ,yet it has limited number of Higher Education Institutes and DAI's that is only 8.

The massive urbanization and ever-increasing population warrants to establish more Higher Education institutes at Urban and Rural areas so that rural population may seek higher Education at Graduate and Post Graduate level at their hometown and head to Bigger cities for Research-based advance Education such as M.Phil, PhD, M.E, D.E etc. This will greatly help in minimizing overcrowding in Higher Education Institutes as you all know that quantity affects the quality of Education.

The Recent statistics show that after Census 2017 that Pakistan needs more Universities, Schools and colleges, Hospitals for People to accommodate and facilitate.

The Demand of Higher Education has been ever increasing

and several Higher Education Institutes both in Public and Private Sector are being established in urban areas but the rural areas are deprived of Higher Education Institutes.

If we take a look at Higher Education Institutes at Division level in Sindh, We will come to know that Larkana Division has a One Medical University , One Engineering College, One General University Campus of Sindh University at Larkana city only, A New Campus of SALU has been established at Shahdadkot , Shikarpur to accommodate the Rural and Population of population of about 6192380 of Division Larkana . There is no any Higher Education Institute at District Level, especially in District Kashmore and Jacobabad.

It is also ironic that as per Census 2017, District Kashmore has the population of 1089169, yet there is only single Degree College at Kandhkot for Three Tehseels i.e. Kandhkot, Kashmore and Kandhkot. Fortunately, a new Degree college has recently been established at Karampur but that too is without SNE may take a year to function properly .

More Over ,The province of Punjab Tops with Maximum number of Universities and Degree Awarding Institutes DAI's with 60 both in Public and Private Sector , followed by Sindh with 55 HEI's in Public and Private Sector , KP with 35 Number of HEI's in Public and Private Sector and fourthly only 8 Universities in Baluchistan .

Additionally, there are 7 universities in Azad Jammu & Kashmir out of which One university namely Al-Khair University has been banned for Degree Verification. It is worthy to mention here that there are 20 universities in Federal Capital

Islamabad.

HEC website also shows that there total 186 Universities /DAI's to accommodate students from the population of 20,77,74,520 of Pakistan. The 186 HEI's/DAI's are just salt in flour for ever-increasing population of Pakistan since we need more HEI's and DAI's .

It is also an irony that from 186 HEI's and DAI's, most of HEI's and DAI's are established at Big cities such as Karachi with 41, Lahore with 34, Islamabad with 20 respectively. The Number shows that most of these HEI's and DAI's are available to Urban Population whereas Rural Population has only limited chances for getting admission in Medical, Engineering College or General University in comparison to Urban Population.

This divide is further aggravated when the need arises for a Professional Accountancy Institutes such as Institute of Chartered Accountants of Pakistan (ICAP) Karachi and Institute of Management Accountants of Pakistan (ICMAP) Karachi. These Accountancy specific Institutes are available for Urban Population such as the metropolitan city of Karachi only. There may be very few private Accountancy Colleges in other provinces but the authorized Accountancy colleges are only ICAP and ICMAP offering CA, ICMA Degree for Accounting and Auditing Professionals.

It is also recommended that ICAP and ICMAP should establish their campuses at other cities to facilitate the rural Population to extend Higher Education outreach. Furthermore, the HEC 's plan to establish District based campuses of various Medical, Engineering and General University campuses is a good initiative but the question arises that whether these campuses will impart the same level of Standardized Education as these do at their main campuses –is a big concern since at campus they will have limited resources, staff and limited Technology to impart Education and will offer only Graduate and Post Graduate Degrees .

It is also the great concern that most of the campuses are established without need-based analysis and influenced by Political will. Such campuses fail to cater to the needs of the community. HEC should personally monitor the Campuses Establishment, keeping in view the Population Needs and Requirements for such HEI or DAI campus.

The HEC should also expedite the process of Proposed HEI's and DAI's campuses so that drop out ratio may be minimized after Intermediate. Especially, the upper Sindh i.e. Sukkur and Larkana Division may have more HEI's and DAI's especially Medical, Engineering and General Universities since Sukkur is 3rd Biggest City of Sindh having no any General university Except the IBA-Sukkur.

District Kashmore immediately requires two Degree Colleges for Both boys and Girls and a General university Campus , an Engineering College and a Medical College to cater to the needs of 1089169 Population and the bordering Districts of Punjab i.e Rajanpur and Dera Bugti District of Baluchistan as Kashmore is Gateway to Sindh for People coming from Punjab and Baluchistan province .

It is very important to know that If our Rulers want to build the nation then Higher Education is necessary to impart professional Education and enable the people to do research in multiple fields and build the foundations Knowledge Driven Economy .

9

Political Instability in PML-N Regime

It has been almost one and half year of PML (N) led Federal Government to complete but the situation is going from bad to verse. On the Economic front , it has achieved a tremendous success but on the Security front, it has been facing the constant internal and External threats . The Bomb blasts , extortion and Communal riots are on the rise and the whole country is going through the most dangerous and critical security situation which shows no sign of improvement .

Despite failure of dialogue with Tehreek Taliban Pakistan (TTP) after their conditional Ceasefire , So far no positive results have been experienced or observed as reported by the main stream Security analysts . Consequent upon the Presidential Elections in Afghanistan , the deadline of NATO forces withdrawal from Afghanistan is fast approaching and with replacement of Karzai Government , Pakistan will be facing the Security threats from the TTP factions existing in Tribal Areas , Punjab and long bordering Afghanistan . With aggressive attitude of Armed forces after the induction of General Pervez Musharaf in the high treason case of suspending

34

the Constitution and imposing emergency in the country .

The Army as an institution is in aggressive mood as Renowned Analyst and Journalist Najam Sethi has predicted that Army will resist any capital punishment given to Former Chief of Armed Forces General Pervez Musharaf. As the later himself claimed and still claims that the Army is with him. The Statement of general Pervez Musharaf that he enjoys the support from the Armed Forces cannot be ruled out as Political parties have started consultations over giving the safe exit to former Armed Chief to avoid institutional confrontation .

The All of Sudden decision of Armed forces to initiate major Offensive against various factions of Taliban militants under the operation Zarab-e-Azab in North Waziristan and other Tribal Agencies clearly echoes the "all powerful institutional status" of the Armed Forces . The judiciary and The parliament are being overshadowed by the Mighty Institution with the passage of Protection of Pakistan Act 2014 which could be used against the anti state Actors and security personnel could detain any suspect or political Activist for the period of 90 days without reporting the whereabouts of the Detainee.

On other hand , After serious incident of Model Town Lahore which claimed 12 innocent lives and 90 persons got injured, has started a tug of war between the Strong man Shahbaz Shareef and Revolutionary Dr Tahir –ur-Qadri as the later has been criticizing the Punjab Government for bad governance and demanding the case may be registered against Punjab CM and Security Personnel considering them responsible for the Model town Shootout . To remove the stain from Shahbaz

Sharif , Sharif Brothers ousted the Provincial Law minister Rana Sanaullah making him Sacrificial Goat . The Gullu Butt Mystery is yet another issue to be reckoned with. The PML (N) seems to be between devil and deep sea to deal with the issues popping up all of sudden.

The PTI's head Imran Khan's Saga is yet another pressure tool for the government to deal with since Mr. Khan has been demanding recount of four Constituencies of Lahore but the Government has not heeded to them as yet . The Demand has been supported by the PPP recently which might have confused the already under pressure Sharifs to make some tough decisions since PTI's Announcement for Freedom March on 14th August might have compelled the PML (N) government to make some measures to cope with the Freedom March plan .

Asif Ali Zardari's recent statement over PTI's Demand may have shaken the PML (N) leadership since Zardari's PPP enjoys the strong Position in the Assembly as well as in Senate which may create hurdles in the way of PML(N) and may create such a scenario where Midterm Polls looming Possibility , may become a reality as with MQM a coalition partner in Sindh with PPP , both may force the Sharifs to accept the demands and make some bitter Decisions which may change the entire situation .

Pakistan has become the land of controversies such as Dr Arsalan Iftikhar's recent Blame game against PTI chief and challenging the Candidature of Imran Khan and PTI challenging the Candidature of Sharif brothers has other motives to disclose since the parties have been watching the situation very attentively and joint opposition Alliance Possibility could not be ruled out as every Political party has got some Common interest and every party wants to win the hearts of the people with their campaigns against the government .

Some mainstream Parties have initiated campaigns against Rigging , corruption and energy crisis , some have raised issues against operation , some has criticized the privatization road map for the State Institutions ,some have criticized the Economic and Human Rights Policies . Some have also criticized the nepotism and favoritism in the appointment of heads of various State Institutions. So much so, that almost every Political Party has a bone to pick with the Government. In this connection, Government has been compelled by the prevalent situation has decided to let the Freedom Marchers to March on Independence since the PML(N) think tanks have advised the Government that if government resisted to the Freedom Marchers led by Imran Khan , may have serious repercussion which may change the entire scenario and create such situation which may further aggravate the governance and PML(N) led Federal government days may be counted .

The recent Popularity Survey conducted by Gallop and other Organization show that PTI enjoys the First Position , PPP second and the PML(N) has slipped to number three as PML(N)'s popularity graph has been constantly maintaining downward trend which is not suitable for already criticized party by the leaders of mainstream party . The People of Pakistan has been fed up with "you –n-me" turns and want this to be changed with performance indicators and visionary leadership. The people have become fatigued to elect same legislators from the same constituency for consecutive three decades and want the old faces to be replaced with new ones .

As the oldies have become controversial due to corruption , nepotism , favoritism , influence on security agencies and other state machineries and inefficiency and lack of clear policy and vision to materialize the promise they had made with the people during their Election campaigns or those written in their Election Manifestos .Election manifestos are written to attract the voters to cast their votes in the favor of Parties candidate as nobody takes any responsibility to review the previous manifestos and update the manifestos with clear vision .

For instance , PML(N) had promised to end load shedding in six months but failed miserably and heavily criticized for setting illogical targets without any consultation with Power Sector Specialist or doing any research on any issue since Except the PTI ,No any party has any strategic Policy unit to address the key issues and do some research present and future issues related Human Rights , Development , Planning , Demography , Social Development , Economic Development , Natural Resource Management , Security , foreign Policy , Democracy and Governance and come up with lasting solutions to those issues of higher importance and drafting their manifestos on the basis of Research and Situation analysis rather than just exaggerated calculations and making illogical conclusion which be the basis for criticism at a time when these same issues may become the cause of the Government failure . So why not take some initiative in advance to address the issues and find out lasting solutions after Research, analysis and consultations. This will change the whole picture of the governance and bring in innovations in Democratic Process rather than just traditional Politics .

10

The Positive + Startups in Pakistan

Startups changing the world with the innovations in every type of business . The Entrepreneurs around the World have gathered to rock the World with their innovative ideas . When world is inclined to change then Pakistan cannot be an exception . The Entrepreneurs like Asad Omar and man behind the source of inspiration and CEO of Naseeb Networks , Mr Moonis Rahman have already left the world How a Developing country like Pakistan could tap the resources and Entrepreneurs who are doing wonders in their fields.

There are several reasons for the inspiration of Pakistani Entrepreneurs to come up with innovative ideas and help build the Small Business Company that fuel the Economy of Pakistan at large . let's see what inspired the Pakitreneurs to emerge on the pages of Inc , Forbes and Entrepreneurs Magazines .

1. **Business & Management Institutes** : The Business Institutes such IBA Karachi , Lums , IBA Sukkur , KITE , KSBL etc have nurtured the business graduates and their entrepreneurial institutes have brought out the creative genie among them and provided them with the platform to create ideas and turn them into reality through incubation and

acceleration Centers Such as LUMS center of Entrepreneurship , The Center for Entrepreneurial Development (CED) -IBA Karachi are some of the prominent centers where business graduates are groomed and Ideas are turned into reality through trainings and Grants .

2.**Global Startups Impact** : Startups such as Amazon ,Mashable , Box.net , Google ,Inc , yahoo, MicroSoft etc have really played the key role to attract the young Entrepreneurs . Their Sales , Marketing ,Finance and profit details prompted the Entrepreneurs including Pakistani Entrepreneurs to start their own E-Businesses .

3. **Government backed Incubation Centers** : Finally , Offical launch of Plan9 & Plan X has surfaced . Plan9 is the Pakistan's first technology startup incubation program which is being run by the Punjab Information Technology Board (PITB). Plan9 is the greatest Program to provide space, mentor ship, electricity (yes, electricity), and legal support for startups who are incubated. Like Business institutes IBA ,LUMS , Plan 9 & Plan X have attracted the Youth and they (youth) successfully launched their Startups .

4.**Private or Independent Incubators** : Before the Official launch of Government backed incubators ,there were only the Private Sector or Independent incubators who really fueled the Startups and helped the entrepreneurs to Start their business . There are Several Independent incubators but the prominent incubators are : Ivest to innovate I2I is the great Incubator having Startups Savaree , Dheere etc .Net I/O P@SHA's Incubator supported by Global partners such as Google for Entrepreneurs .

5. **The Smartphone Market and Broadband Revolution** : Pakistanis are lucky to have 3G and 4G Spectrums at last .

The Next generation Internet Services have transformed the nation and the focus has been shifted to the Technology Driven Startups , IOS and Android APPs etc . With rising demand of Smartphones Android and IOS , Startups have already started reaping the benefits and the figure is expected to go up as the time goes by and with permission from Google Play store to allow Wallet accounts for Pakistani to Sell their APPs globally . With over 14 crore Mobile phone users , the figure is go up and will facilitate the the Small business Investors to reap benefits as 3G and 4G grounds all over Pakistan in next couple of years .

It is high time for Government specially the Ministry of IT and Telecom at Federal Level and IT departments at Provincial , Division and District Level to devise policies to help boost Startup culture and Establish Business Incubation and Acceleration Centers to encourage young Entrepreneurs of Colleges and universities or Even Schools to Turn their Dream into reality and help the country in Economic Development , Eradication of Poverty and Unemployment .The Startups will help in creating jobs and contribute to Social and Economic Development .

11

Reshaping Foreign Policy Initiative

Pakistan's Foreign Policy has always remained the Arab Centric with Saudi Arab having Central role and Even its alignment towards the US since Independence. Pakistan has never revisited its Foreign Policy holistically to suit the Needs of the country on independent approach. Since Independence, Pakistan has never clarified its stance on Foreign Policy development and the Terms of Engagement with its neighbours and the big powers. That was why Pakistan's First Prime Minister Liaquat Ali Khan Preferred the US than Russia for its Friendship and paid his visit to America and became the part of West Block than East Block ie the then USSR.

Though Pakistan played a pivotal role in Russia-Afghan war but this strategic partnership did not bear any fruit for the nation due to Political instability, Strong Military Intervention and weak fiscal Policies. This Diplomatic relationship or bonhomie has never proved Fruitful for the country owing to America being a fair weather Friend as Pak-US relations have always been marred by Distrust .Even Security Aid offered to Pakistan by America affected its Independent Foreign Policy to the extent that the used aid as pressure tool to force Pakistan to do More to combat terrorism and remove Safe haven of terrorists within Pakistan Domain . Although, Pakistan laid down numerous sacrifices of Soldiers and Civilians; approximately over 100000 in so-called War against Terrorism. Pakistan has already paid a heavy price to be an Ally of Pakistan .

Especially, American led NATO strikes on Afghanistan in which Pakistan was asked to cooperate and hand over the Airports and Roads for Transportation of weapons to Afghanistan for NATO forces to topple Taliban Government and to kill or capture Osama Bin Ladin -The Master Mind of 9/11 Strike on World Trade Centre. American president Bush attacked Afghanistan to avenge the 9/11 incident and to please his fellow Americans. Ever since the Strike, Afghanistan is still unstable despite the passage of 17 years of American led NATO Forces Presence.Even Taliban control 40 % of Afghanistan till today . There is no peace and frequents Suicide attacks on NATO forces and civilians have become the order of the day .

America is losing the Afghan war against terrorism badly but it resorts to blame Pakistan for Terrorist Safe Haves along the Durand line and its fiasco in Afghan War is being associated with Pakistan but the statistics suggest that Pakistan has suffered a lot than the US. Hundreds of Civilians and Soldiers were killed in Suicide Bomb blasts on Mosques, Churches, Temples, Schools and other Political Rallies.

This happened because Pakistan cooperated with the US in Afghanistan allowing it to use Pakistan's soil against Taliban . Such cooperation enraged Taliban against Pakistan and they become fierce enemies of Pakistan - especially its brave Armed forces who initiated their major offensive against these Extremists in shape of Operation Zarb-e-Azb and Operation

Rad-ul-Fassad which broke their Waist and Pakistan returned to peace . The Pak-Aghan border became the route for Aghan Taliban to penetrate in KPK and Punjab. Our Political Parties have never mandated the Security agencies against such extremist forces owing to their close linkages with them by a few political parties who have never condemned these elements rather supported them privately. After APS attack, Political parties gave go head to Paramilitary forces to launch Operation after adopting National Action Plan and establishing NACTA.

Pakistan Army has given unprecedented sacrifices for the defence of the country but Americans remained stuck to do more and same narrative of "Do More" prompted American President Donald Trump to blame Pakistan Through tweet that Pakistan has deceived US despite being paid billions in Security Aid. That blame stirred widespread protests against Us in Pakistan by various Parties. Even, ISPR Chief Major General Asif Ghafoor said that the aid they received is just $225 Million, not Billion.Even, the then PML-N Government was on the same page with ISPR and decided to review and reshape their Policy with new and equal terms of Engagement with the US but unfortunately that did not materialize since it was too late for them to respond as there was no Foreign Minister in PML-N Government for almost four years, only Sartaj Aziz worked as Advisor to PM on Foreign Affairs . Pakistan did fail in devising an independent foreign Policy due to being the recipient of Security aid from the US and they stood Mum over the issue for several days until the regular debate on Electronic Media compelled them clarify and respond to the allegationa that rocked the country's supremacy and Respect amongst world Nations.

Now, when PTI has emerged as Single majority Party at Centre and likely to form Govt in Center ,Punjab, KPK and Coalition Government in Baluchistan , It has great opportunity to devise an independent Foreign Policy for Pakistan to boost up its image Internationally and building Trade ties with neighbours. In his Victory Speech, Imran Khan envisaged his Foreign Policy that he intends to extend trade links and economic connectivity in the region and beyond. In the Foreign Policy of PTI led Government, Saudi Arab and Iran will have central role followed by Old friend China. He resolved to maintain friendly relations with China and continue the CPEC projects for Infrastructural Development of Pakistan. He said that relationship with Saudi Arab and Iran will benefit Pakistan on ideological grounds and help improve Pakistan economically.

He also Envisaged US-Pak Relations on equality basis which may be beneficial for both Nations rather than the imposition over other. Especially, Imran Khan's interests in maintaining Stability in Afghanistan as except this, there would be looming security threats for Pakistan. Pakistan envisages engagement with Washington on equality basis and as a key ally to the US on basis of Mutual interest and trust.

He aspired that there should be peace in Afghanistan so that we have open borders with Afghanistan for trade as Afghanistan is a landlocked Country and it has only option to have traded through Pakistan.

About relations with India, he had the clear position that Pakistan wants Trade with India and other neighbours but the Kashmir issue has the central role. He offered India for dialogue to discuss the issue on Table Talks rather than indulging in Blame Game for Internal incidents. He stressed that the trade between Pakistan and India will mutually benefit both countries. Since PTI's main objective is to revive the Pakistan economy and decrease the growing foreign Debt and boosting and attracting investments in the country. He went on to say that If India advances one Step forward, I would advance two steps as it is very important for the people of Kashmir that the issue must be resolved through Dialogue to pave the way for the trade .

Let's hope that if PTI led Government reshapes the Foreign Policy of Pakistan and the Terms of Engagement with Neighbors and big powers i.e US, China and Russia , it will have far-reaching effects and Pakistan will reap the benefits of Regional Connectivity and revival of Economy provided that the New envisioned Policy is implemented in letter and spirit . Since it is the right time to do every possible attempt and utilize every possible option to revive the economy and bringing in foreign investments and getting rid of foreign Debt.

Imran Khan's Foreign Policy Vision has been welcomed by the world especially Saudi Arab, Iran, India, US, China and Afghanistan and all the countries showed their resolve to extend bilateral relations with New PTI Government of Pakistan. Even, Afghan President, Ashraf Ghani through his tweet confirmed that he had Telephonic conversation with Imran Khan and have extended the invitation to Imran Khan to pay his kind Visit to Afghanistan and reiterated his stance to extend bilateral relations. Similar gesture was also shown by Saudi Arab, Iran, China, US and India through their Ambassadors and foreign Office Spokesmen.

There is also a plan in the ranks of PTI to invite all the SAARC Member Nations" PMs ,Presidents including Indian

PM Narendra Modi , Afghan President ,Ashraf Ghani , Saudi Arab Prince , Turkish President Erdogan to participate in oath taking ceremony of Imran Khan as PM of Pakistan but PTI's spokesman Mehmood-ul Rashid confirmed that such development is in pipeline and it will be discussed in the meeting after the process of formation of Governments in center, Punjab and KP .

12

Foreign Policy under Imran Khan's Premiership

Now, when PTI has emerged as Single majority Party at Centre and likely to form Govt in Center ,Punjab, KPK and Coalition Government in Baluchistan , It has great opportunity to devise an independent Foreign Policy for Pakistan to boost up its image Internationally and building Trade ties with neighbours. In his Victory Speech, Imran Khan envisaged his Foreign Policy that he intends to extend trade links and economic connectivity in the region and beyond. In the Foreign Policy of PTI led Government, Saudi Arab and Iran will have central role followed by Old friend China. He resolved to maintain friendly relations with China and continue the CPEC projects for Infrastructural Development of Pakistan. He said that relationship with Saudi Arab and Iran will benefit Pakistan on ideological grounds and help improve Pakistan economically.

He also Envisaged US-Pak Relations on equality basis which may be beneficial for both Nations rather than the imposition over other. Especially, Imran Khan's interests in maintaining

Stability in Afghanistan as except this, there would be looming security threats for Pakistan. Pakistan envisages engagement with Washington on equality basis and as a key ally to the US on basis of Mutual interest and trust.

He aspired that there should be peace in Afghanistan so that we have open borders with Afghanistan for trade as Afghanistan is a landlocked Country and it has only option to have traded through Pakistan.

About relations with India, he had the clear position that Pakistan wants Trade with India and other neighbours but the Kashmir issue has the central role. He offered India for dialogue to discuss the issue on Table Talks rather than indulging in Blame Game for Internal incidents. He stressed that the trade between Pakistan and India will mutually benefit both countries. Since PTI's main objective is to revive the Pakistan economy and decrease the growing foreign Debt and boosting and attracting investments in the country. He went on to say that If India advances one Step forward, I would advance two steps as it is very important for the people of Kashmir that the issue must be resolved through Dialogue to pave the way for the trade .

Let's hope that if PTI led Government reshapes the Foreign Policy of Pakistan and the Terms of Engagement with Neighbors and big powers i.e US, China and Russia , it will have far-reaching effects and Pakistan will reap the benefits of Regional Connectivity and revival of Economy provided that the New envisioned Policy is implemented in letter and spirit . Since it is the right time to do every possible attempt and utilize every possible option to revive the economy and bringing in foreign investments and getting rid of foreign Debt.

Imran Khan's Foreign Policy Vision has been welcomed by the world especially Saudi Arab, Iran, India, US, China and Afghanistan and all the countries showed their resolve to extend bilateral relations with New PTI Government of Pakistan. Even, Afghan President, Ashraf Ghani through his tweet confirmed that he had Telephonic conversation with Imran Khan and have extended the invitation to Imran Khan to pay his kind Visit to Afghanistan and reiterated his stance to extend bilateral relations. Similar gesture was also shown by Saudi Arab, Iran, China, US and India through their Ambassadors and foreign Office Spokesmen.

There is also a plan in the ranks of PTI to invite all the SAARC Member Nations" PMs ,Presidents including Indian PM Narendra Modi , Afghan President ,Ashraf Ghani , Saudi Arab Prince , Turkish President Erdogan to participate in oath taking ceremony of Imran Khan as PM of Pakistan but PTI's spokesman Mehmood-ul Rashid confirmed that such development is in pipeline and it will be discussed in the meeting after the process of formation of Governments in center, Punjab and KP .

13

Challenges Before New PM Imran Khan

With PTI Emerging as single Majority Party having more than 115 NA seats and More than 124 PA seats in Punjab, 65 PA seats in KP and Second Major Party in Sindh with 22 PA Seats, PTI Chairman is well prepared to be the Prime Minister of Pakistan. The Idea of "Naya Pakistan" worked and people left their comfort zone and voted for change. After, overall seat analysis, PTI is well in position to form Government in Center, Punjab and KP.While PML-N 62 NA Seats , 130 PA seats of Punjab and PPP as third with 39 NA seats and 68 PA seats of Sindh and will like form government in Sindh . Furthermore , PTI will sit on Opposition benches in Sindh possibly giving tough time to PPPP to improve their performance Since MQM was bit humble or friendly with PPP as the City Mayor Belonged to their Party in the previous tenure .

In today's Public address, PTI Chief (Future PM) said that he was the only leader ever to be targeted personally but buried all rifts , the differences and has completely wiped out his Past differences with people. He further clarified that he will not pursue the Policy of Victimization either.He projected his clear vision that he will establish close brotherly relations with All the major Islamic Countries Especially Saudi Arabia, Iran, Turkey and will play his role to diffuse tensions between Saudi Arab and Iran. He stressed that the rule of law to be the top priority before his Government.

He was reported as saying that PTI government will focus on Education, Health, Police Reforms, Job creation, Fiscal Policy, Foreign Policy and Best Governance Model that suits the Democratic Trend and the Model of Pakistan. He specially hinted to involve 200 Pakistanis working abroad to reform the institutions to be made functional on modern Lines. The first Challenge to PTI is the implementation of Uniform Education Policy in all the four provinces. It is suggested that Education to be made Federal Subject to have uniformity in Curriculum and its foundation on international Standards. Secondly, the promotion of Scientific Research and Technology in all the Four provinces including GB.

The Establishment of New Universities throughout Pakistan in the Lines of NAMAL college Mianwali. The Scholarships many be offered to the Deserving students so that they may face the problem of lack Funds for Studies. Establishing and creating Job Markets so that the university graduates may not face problem in getting jobs. Offering Scholarships for M.Phil and Ph.D Members of public Universities as well as for the talented Students to further their research in their respective fields.

The Establishment of New Hospitals in each Taluka Head Quarter and District Head Quarters and up gradation of existing Hospitals and equipping them with Modern facilities.

Establishment of Cancer Hospital in every province to facilitate the Cancer patients and ensure their treatment free of Cost. Introducing Health cards or Insurance for the patients with Fatal diseases. The Health insurance will cover their treatment costs. The Energy crisis has been very critical in Pakistan due to Demand and Supply GAP. PTI has to spearhead the Construction of New Dams such as Bhasha and Mohammad Dams since these have been cleared by Chief Justice of Pakistan ,Justice Saquib Nisar that need to be constructed on Public-Private Node.

He even established the Dams Construction Fund. PTI can further the fundraising so that construction work must be started on time. The load-shedding problem is very old even PML-N has not resolved the Load shedding issue. As the PML-N leadership, Nawaz Shareef and Shahbaz Shareef told white lies with the Simple people Pakistan that the issue of Load shedding will be resolved by 2018 but people of Pakistan are still experiencing Load unresolved. PTI has to solve the core issue on war footing basis so that prosperity could be brought in Pakistan and the Textile & Garments Industry of Karachi and Faisalabad could be revitalized.

The third biggest challenge is the depreciation of Rupee against Dollar. The Economist team should be engaged with the composition of Senior and young economists and to do the spade work for viable and sustainable Economic policy. In this connection, the services of Policy Think Tanks specially Sustainable Development Policy Institute (SDPI) Islamabad would be the key to give the best policy advise and great Professional Asad Umar would be Instrumental in this regard as well.

The Fourth Biggest challenge is the devising of Internal policy and Foreign Policy for Pakistan . it is imperative that Pakistan should adopt a clear foreign Policy and determine new terms of Engagement with US, Russia and our old friend neighbour China. Execution and acceleration of CPEC Projects must improve the Infrastructure of Pakistan.

The Fifth biggest challenge is to gain access to International Markets to improve and increase exports of Pakistan such as Grains, Fruits, Textiles and Garments. Establishing Industrial Zones and Economic zones and functioning of Gawadar Port. The Improvement of Communication, Highways, Railways and Airways especially restructuring of PIA and Pakistan Steel.

The Sixth largest challenge is the Governance Model especially the Local Governance. This should be a federal subject so that there should be a uniform local governance Model. The Experts should be engaged to study the standard local Governance Models and adopt or devise the models given needs and requirements local People .

There is also the issue of security at Loc with India owing to The Kashmir Dispute. Even the so-called Indian Media dubbed the Victory of Imran Khan as a bad omen for India due to their bonhomie with PML-N. PML-N has always maintained friendly relations with the compromise on the Kashmir. In this connection, PTI initiatives to highlight the issue in the light of UN for its resolution .

If all these issues are resolved, the people of Pakistan will have the positive image about PTI and its visionary leadership. People have trusted PTI leadership and Hopefully, PTI won't breach the trust.

People Voted for the Change and they just want to reap the fruits of change and see Pakistan as the country where the unemployment, security issues, Education issues , Health issues, bad Governance should be wiped as per their Slogan of *Naya Pakistan*.

There should be zero tolerance for corruption and The Institutions such as NAB, ACE and FIA may take action against any person if he is found involved with clear evidence.

There should also be strict laws for Corruption and befitting punishment will be meted out as was done with former PM Nawaz and his Daughter Mariam Safdar and Captain Safdar.

It is clear from their sentence that no matter how powerful the corrupt people are, they would be executed in a similar fashion. There should be a congenial environment for the Foreign Direct Investment FDI and the boosting of the Hotel and Tourism Industry as done by UAE and Malaysia etc. Hope IK will fulfill his promises and solve the Challenges of Pakistan with dedicated and professional team.